MW01001011

Transformation

Rebecca Manley Pippert

with Dale and Sandy Larsen

6 STUDIES FOR INDIVIDUALS OR GROUPS
WITH LEADER'S NOTES

Inter-Varsity Press
Nottingham, England

IVP Connect
An imprint of InterVarsity Press
Downers Grove, Illinois

InterVarsity Press, USA
P.O. Box 1400, Downers Grove, IL 60515-1426, USA
World Wide Web: www.ivpress.com
Email: email@ivpress.com

Inter-Varsity Press, England
Norton Street, Nottingham NG7 3HR, England
World Wide Web: www.ivpbooks.com
Email: ivp@ivpbooks.com

InterVarsity Press®, U.S.A., is the book-publishing division of InterVarsity Christian Fellowship/USA®, a student movement active on campus at hundreds of universities, colleges and schools of nursing in the United States of America, and a member movement of the International Fellowship of Evangelical Students. For information about local and regional activities, write Public Relations Dept., InterVarsity Christian Fellowship/ USA, 6400 Schroeder Rd., P.O. Box 7895, Madison, WI 53707-7895, or visit the IVCF website at <www.intervarsity.org>.

This study guide is based on and adapts material from A Heart for God by Rebecca Manley Pippert © 1996.

Inter-Varsity Press, England, is the book-publishing division of the Universities and Colleges Christian Fellowship (formerly the Inter-Varsity Fellowship), a student movement linking Christian Unions in universities and colleges throughout the United Kingdom and the Republic of Ireland, and a member movement of the International Fellowship of Evangelical Students. For information about local and national activities write to UCCF, 38 De Montfort Street, Leicester LE1 7GP.

All Scripture quotations, unless otherwise indicated, are taken from the Holy Bible, New International Version®. NIV®. Copyright © 1973, 1978, 1984 by International Bible Society. Used by permission of Zondervan Publishing House. Distributed in the U.K. by permission of Hodder and Stoughton Ltd. All rights reserved. "NIV" is a registered trademark of International Bible Society. UK trademark number 1448790.

Cover design: Cindy Kiple; cover photograph: Melanie Acevedo/Photonica

USA ISBN 978-0-8308-2019-1

UK ISBN 978-0-85111-356-2

Printed in the United States of America ∞

P	19	18	17	16	15	14	13	12	11	10	9	8	7	6	5
Y	21	20	19	18	17	16	15	14	13	12	11	10	09		

CONTENTS

GETTING THE MOST OUT OF
Christian Basics Bible Studies

Knowing Christ is where faith begins. From there we grow through the essentials of discipleship: Bible study, prayer, Christian community and much more. We learn to set godly priorities, grow in Christian character and witness to others. We persevere through doubts and grow in wisdom. These are the topics woven into each of the Christian Basics Bible Studies. Working through this series will help you become a more mature Christian.

WHAT KIND OF GUIDE IS THIS?

The studies are not designed to merely tell you what one person thinks. Instead, through inductive study, they will help you discover for yourself what Scripture is saying. Each study deals with a particular passage—rather than jumping around the Bible—so that you can really delve into the author's meaning in that context.

The studies ask three different kinds of questions. *Observation* questions help you to understand the content of the passage by asking about the basic facts: who, what, when, where and how. *Interpretation* questions delve into the meaning of the passage. *Application* questions help you discover its implications for growing in Christ.

These three keys unlock the treasures of the biblical writings and help you live them out.

This is a thought-provoking guide. Each question assumes a variety of answers. Many questions do not have "right" answers, particularly questions that aim at meaning or application. Instead, the questions should inspire users to explore the passage more thoroughly.

This study guide is flexible. You can use it for individual study, but it is also great for a variety of groups—student, professional, neighborhood or church groups. Each study takes about forty-five minutes in a group setting or thirty minutes in personal study.

HOW THEY'RE PUT TOGETHER

Each study is composed of four sections: opening paragraphs and questions to help you get into the topic, the NIV text and questions that invite study of the passage, questions to help you apply what you have learned, and a suggestion for prayer.

The workbook format provides space for writing a response to each question. This format is ideal for personal study and allows group members to prepare in advance for the discussion and/or write down notes during the study. This space can form a permanent record of your thoughts and spiritual progress.

At the back of the guide are study notes that may be useful for leaders or for individuals. These notes do not give "the answers," but they do provide additional background information on certain questions to help you through the difficult spots. The "Guidelines for Leaders" section describes how to lead a group discussion, gives helpful tips on group dynamics and suggests ways to deal with problems that may arise during the discussion. With such helps, someone with little or no experience can lead an effective group study.

SUGGESTIONS FOR INDIVIDUAL STUDY

1. This guide is based on a classic book or booklet that will enrich your spiritual life. If you have not read the book or booklet suggested in the "Further Reading" section, you may want to read the portion suggested before you begin your study. The ideas in the book will enhance your study, but the Bible text will be the focus of each session.

2. Read the introduction. Consider the opening questions and note your responses.

3. Pray, asking God to speak to you from his Word about this particular topic.

4. Read the passage reproduced for you from the New International Version. You may wish to mark phrases that seem important. Note in the margin any questions that come to your mind as you read.

5. Use the questions from the study guide to more thoroughly examine the passage. Note your findings in the space provided. After you have made your own notes, read the corresponding study notes in the back of the book for further insights.

6. Reread the entire passage, making further notes about its general principles and about the way you intend to use them.

7. Move to the "Commit" section. Spend time prayerfully considering what the passage has to say specifically to your life.

8. Read the suggestion for prayer. Speak to God about insights you have gained. Tell him of any desires you have for specific growth. Ask him to help you as you attempt to live out the principles described in that passage.

SUGGESTIONS FOR MEMBERS OF A GROUP STUDY

Joining a Bible study group can be a great avenue to spiritual growth. Here are a few guidelines that will help you as you participate in the studies in this guide.

1. Reading the book suggested as further reading, before or after each session, will enhance your study and understanding of the themes in this guide.

2. These studies focus on a particular passage of Scripture—in depth. Only rarely should you refer to other portions of the Bible, and then only at the request of the leader. Of course, the Bible is internally consistent. Other good forms of study draw on that consistency, but inductive Bible study sticks with a single passage and works on it in depth.

3. These are discussion studies. Questions in this guide aim at helping a group discuss together a passage of Scripture in order to understand its content, meaning and implications. Most people are either natural talkers or natural listeners, yet this type of study works best if people participate more or less evenly. Try to curb any natural tendency to either excessive talking or excessive quiet. You and the rest of the group will benefit.

4. Most questions in this guide allow for a variety of answers. If you disagree with someone else's comment, gently say so. Then explain your own point of view from the passage before you.

5. Be willing to lead a discussion, if asked. Much of the preparation for leading has already been accomplished in the writing of this guide.

6. Respect the privacy of people in your group. Many people speak

of things within the context of a Bible study/prayer group that they do not want to be public knowledge. Assume that personal information spoken within the group setting is private, unless you are specifically told otherwise. And don't talk about it elsewhere.

7. We recommend that all groups follow a few basic guidelines and that these guidelines be read at the first session. The guidelines, which you may wish to adapt to your situation, are the following:

a. Anything said in this group is considered confidential and will not be discussed outside the group unless specific permission is given to do so.

b. We will provide time for each person present to talk if he or she feels comfortable doing so.

c. We will talk about ourselves and our own situations, avoiding conversation about other people.

d. We will listen attentively to each other.

e. We will pray for each other.

8. Enjoy your study. Prepare to grow.

SUGGESTIONS FOR GROUP LEADERS

There are specific suggestions to help you in leading in the "Guidelines for Leaders" and in the "Study Notes" at the back of this guide. Read the "Guidelines for Leaders" carefully, even if you are only leading one group meeting. Then you can go to the section on the particular session you will lead.

A Heart for God

For as long as I can remember, I have been deeply drawn to the biblical person of David. His passionate love for God, earthy spirituality and uncompromising humanity speak to me, as they have to believers throughout the centuries.

During a very difficult and painful time in my life, I was drawn once again to reread the books of 1 and 2 Samuel, where the story of David is found. As I read the narrative and also spent time in the Psalms, I found that David gave voice to the entire range of human experience. He prayed with raw honesty, and he came to God empty-handed, offering nothing but his desperate faith. Through the process, God strengthened his faith, deepened his character and transformed David's pain into praise. We learn that no part of our humanity is alien to God's saving work in our lives.

At first glance, the story of David seems to be anything but a morality tale. We see human cunning and pathology. We see people lie, envy, hate, murder. But we also see what happens when people open themselves and respond to God, and how their moral character is formed and shaped over time.

We know more about David than almost any other person in the Bible. Besides being an exemplary ruler, he was a military and political genius, a poet of exceptional skill, a talented musician, and the architect who designed the temple that his son Solomon built. Usually a person that gifted intimidates us. Yet people genuinely loved and were drawn to David.

Why is he still so appealing even thousands of years later? I asked a friend what came to her mind when she thought of the biblical David. "Human!" she answered in a flash. Her answer was on target. Larger-than-life, passionate and gifted though David was, what draws us to him is his humanity. As we read his psalms, we realize that he not only understood our feelings but shared them. As we read the central events of his life, the progression from shepherd boy to king of Israel, we feel he was one of us.

In the life of David we see how God used the choices and crises of David's life to transform his character and shape him into the person God wanted him to be. The good news is that God will do the same in our lives, if we are willing to let him. It is my hope that as we encounter David in the following studies, we will come face to face with this extraordinary man from the Bible—and that in doing so, we will come face to face with who *we* are. But more than anything, I hope that we will encounter the living God and by his grace be transformed into the people he would have us to be, people with hearts like his.

From Fear to Faith
1 Samuel 17:1-50

Most of us are plagued with fears and doubts that outsiders would not believe even if we told them.

The silver lining in the dark cloud of fear is that fear pushes us to decide on our view of reality. What do I truly believe about the universe? Am I alone in this battle, or is there a God who over-rules human affairs? One need only experience real fear once to know that it matters desperately whether there is a divine power outside of ourselves that can neutralize and overcome any present danger.

Saul behaved as if God was irrelevant to the battle. David had a different perception of the battle because he saw it as theolog-ically rooted. As far as David was concerned, life's difficulties al-ways present us with a choice. Do we trust in appearances or in the unseen living God? For David there was no contest, because he was convinced that beyond appearances lay the deeper reality of God.

No matter what life looks like presently, no matter how much it appears that evil is winning, humans don't have the last word. God has the last word, and it is a word of hope, peace and victory to those who love him and are walking in his will.

OPEN

- What is something which you once feared, but are not afraid of any longer?

What has made the difference?

- How does fear distort our view of God?

 STUDY

Read 1 Samuel 17:1-50.

¹Now the Philistines gathered their forces for war. . . . ³The Philistines occupied one hill and the Israelites another, with the valley between them.

⁴A champion named Goliath, who was from Gath, came out of

the Philistine camp. He was over nine feet tall. [5]He had a bronze helmet on his head and wore a coat of scale armor of bronze weighing five thousand shekels; [6]on his legs he wore bronze greaves, and a bronze javelin was slung on his back. [7]His spear shaft was like a weaver's rod, and its iron point weighed six hundred shekels. His shield bearer went ahead of him.

[8]Goliath stood and shouted to the ranks of Israel, "Why do you come out and line up for battle? Am I not a Philistine, and are you not the servants of Saul? Choose a man and have him come down to me. [9]If he is able to fight and kill me, we will become your subjects; but if I overcome him and kill him, you will become our subjects and serve us." [10]Then the Philistine said, "This day I defy the ranks of Israel! Give me a man and let us fight each other." [11]On hearing the Philistine's words, Saul and all the Israelites were dismayed and terrified.

[12]Now David was the son of an Ephrathite named Jesse, who was from Bethlehem in Judah. Jesse had eight sons, and in Saul's time he was old and well advanced in years. [13]Jesse's three oldest sons had followed Saul to the war: The firstborn was Eliab; the second, Abinadab; and the third, Shammah. [14]David was the youngest. The three oldest followed Saul, [15]but David went back and forth from Saul to tend his father's sheep at Bethlehem.

[16]For forty days the Philistine came forward every morning and evening and took his stand.

[17]Now Jesse said to his son David, "Take this ephah of roasted grain and these ten loaves of bread for your brothers and hurry to their camp. [18]Take along these ten cheeses to the commander of their unit. See how your brothers are and bring back some assurance from them. [19]They are with Saul and all the men of Israel in the Valley of Elah, fighting against the Philistines."

[20]Early in the morning David left the flock with a shepherd, loaded up and set out, as Jesse had directed. He reached the camp as the army was going out to its battle positions, shouting the war cry. [21]Israel and the Philistines were drawing up their lines facing each other. [22]David left his things with the keeper of supplies, ran to the battle lines and greeted his brothers. [23]As he was talking with them, Goliath, the Philistine champion from Gath, stepped out from his lines and shouted his usual defiance, and David heard it. [24]When the Israelites saw the man, they all ran from him in great fear.

[25]Now the Israelites had been saying, "Do you see how this man keeps coming out? He comes out to defy Israel. The king will give great wealth to the man who kills him. He will also give him his daughter in marriage and will exempt his father's family from taxes in Israel."

[26]David asked the men standing near him, "What will be done for the man who kills this Philistine and removes this disgrace from Israel? Who is this uncircumcised Philistine that he should defy the armies of the living God?"

[27]They repeated to him what they had been saying and told him, "This is what will be done for the man who kills him."

[28]When Eliab, David's oldest brother, heard him speaking with the men, he burned with anger at him and asked, "Why have you come down here? And with whom did you leave those few sheep in the desert? I know how conceited you are and how wicked your heart is; you came down only to watch the battle."

[29]"Now what have I done?" said David. "Can't I even speak?" [30]He then turned away to someone else and brought up the same matter, and the men answered him as before. [31]What David said was overheard and reported to Saul, and Saul sent for him.

[32]David said to Saul, "Let no one lose heart on account of this

Philistine; your servant will go and fight him."

³³Saul replied, "You are not able to go out against this Philistine and fight him; you are only a boy, and he has been a fighting man from his youth."

³⁴But David said to Saul, "Your servant has been keeping his father's sheep. When a lion or a bear came and carried off a sheep from the flock, ³⁵I went after it, struck it and rescued the sheep from its mouth. When it turned on me, I seized it by its hair, struck it and killed it. ³⁶Your servant has killed both the lion and the bear; this uncircumcised Philistine will be like one of them, because he has defied the armies of the living God. ³⁷The LORD who delivered me from the paw of the lion and the paw of the bear will deliver me from the hand of this Philistine."

Saul said to David, "Go, and the LORD be with you."

³⁸Then Saul dressed David in his own tunic. He put a coat of armor on him and a bronze helmet on his head. ³⁹David fastened on his sword over the tunic and tried walking around, because he was not used to them.

"I cannot go in these," he said to Saul, "because I am not used to them." So he took them off. ⁴⁰Then he took his staff in his hand, chose five smooth stones from the stream, put them in the pouch of his shepherd's bag and, with his sling in his hand, approached the Philistine.

⁴¹Meanwhile, the Philistine, with his shield bearer in front of him, kept coming closer to David. ⁴²He looked David over and saw that he was only a boy, ruddy and handsome, and he despised him. ⁴³He said to David, "Am I a dog, that you come at me with sticks?" And the Philistine cursed David by his gods. ⁴⁴"Come here," he said, "and I'll give your flesh to the birds of the air and the beasts of the field!"

⁴⁵David said to the Philistine, "You come against me with sword

and spear and javelin, but I come against you in the name of the
LORD Almighty, the God of the armies of Israel, whom you have defied. [46]This day the LORD will hand you over to me, and I'll strike you
down and cut off your head. Today I will give the carcasses of the
Philistine army to the birds of the air and the beasts of the earth, and
the whole world will know that there is a God in Israel. [47]All those
gathered here will know that it is not by sword or spear that the
LORD saves; for the battle is the LORD's, and he will give all of you
into our hands."

[48]As the Philistine moved closer to attack him, David ran quickly
towards the battle line to meet him. [49]Reaching into his bag and taking
out a stone, he slung it and struck the Philistine on the forehead. The
stone sank into his forehead, and he fell face down on the ground.

[50]So David triumphed over the Philistine with a sling and a
stone; without a sword in his hand he struck down the Philistine
and killed him.

---

1. Most people have some basic idea of the story of David and Go-
    liath. As you read the account from the Bible, what details did
    you notice which you did not know or had forgotten?

---

2. Why had the Philistine army and the Israelite army reached a
    standoff (vv. 1-11)?

3. At the sight and sound of Goliath "Saul and all the Israelites were dismayed and terrified" (v. 11). What other words or phrases would describe the feelings of someone facing a battle with Goliath?

4. How did David wind up at the battle line (vv. 12-24)?

5. While the rewards for killing Goliath were attractive (v. 25), what was David's higher motivation for taking him on (vv. 26, 45-47)?

6. What obstacles did David face before he even got into the battle (vv. 28-39)?

7. How had God built David's faith long before he ever encountered Goliath (vv. 34-37)?

8. Think of a severe test that you have endured or are enduring now. How did the Lord build your faith in preparation for that test?

9. The battle between David and Goliath turned out to be unequal, but not in the way Goliath and all the onlookers expected (vv. 41-50). How did David see the battle differently from everyone else (vv. 45-47)?

10. When has the Lord won a spiritual battle in and through you, when all you had were "five smooth stones" versus "sword and spear and javelin"?

COMMIT

- What are the "Goliaths" in your life right now? As you picture each one, repeat the words of David in 1 Samuel 17:45.

Thank God for faith-building experiences. Pray that you will meet obstacles in his strength, not your own.

For further reading: *Chapters one and two of* A Heart for God.

From Envy to Compassion

1 Samuel 20:30-42

No biblical example reveals the destructive pathos of envy as clearly as Saul's relentless pursuit of David. The biblical narrator offers such a bone-chilling description of Saul's slow progression from consumptive envy into paranoia and madness that it could provide therapists enough material to last a lifetime.

Envy rears its head when we are unable to celebrate the gifts or good fortune of another. Envy is the pain we feel when we perceive that someone possesses some object, quality or status we do not possess. Conquering envy requires us to see it for what it is—a dissatisfaction and lack of contentment with life, leading to anger against God.

In contrast to the envy of King Saul toward David is the compassion of Saul's son Jonathan. Jonathan no doubt wanted very much to be the next king of Israel, but he put aside his own self-interests to do what was in the best interest of David. The Bible tells us that Jonathan felt "one in spirit" with David and he "loved him as himself" (1 Samuel 18:1). That is envy's opposite, not to be in competition against, but in solidarity with. When love is expressed through compassion, it is simply incompatible with envy.

OPEN

■ If envy is so destructive, why is it also so appealing?

■ Recall a time you have been on the receiving end of envy. How did you feel about that situation?

How did you feel about the person who envied you?

STUDY

Background: Saul had become envious of David's military victories and favor among the people (1 Samuel 18:5-9). He even told his son Jonathan, heir to the throne, to kill David, but Jonathan refused and warned David instead (1 Samuel 19:1-2). For a time Saul's jealousy appeared to wane; then he again tried to kill David, but David escaped and arranged with Jonathan to sound out Saul's plans. The two arranged a signal using arrows to indicate whether David was still in danger. If Jonathan indicated that the arrows were beyond the boy, then it would mean David must flee. David hid in the field while Jonathan made excuses for his absence at a festival dinner.

Read 1 Samuel 20:30-42.

[30]Saul's anger flared up at Jonathan and he said to him, "You son of a perverse and rebellious woman! Don't I know that you have sided with the son of Jesse to your own shame and to the shame of the mother who bore you? [31]As long as the son of Jesse lives on this earth, neither you nor your kingdom will be established. Now send and bring him to me, for he must die!"

[32]"Why should he be put to death? What has he done?" Jonathan asked his father. [33]But Saul hurled his spear at him to kill him. Then Jonathan knew that his father intended to kill David.

[34]Jonathan got up from the table in fierce anger; on that second day of the month he did not eat, because he was grieved at his father's shameful treatment of David.

[35]In the morning Jonathan went out to the field for his meeting with David. He had a small boy with him, [36]and he said to the boy, "Run and find the arrows I shoot." As the boy ran, he shot an arrow beyond him. [37]When the boy came to the place where Jonathan's arrow had fallen, Jonathan called out after him, "Isn't the arrow beyond you?" [38]Then he shouted, "Hurry! Go quickly! Don't stop!" The boy picked up the arrow and returned to his master. [39](The boy knew nothing of all this; only Jonathan and David knew.) [40]Then Jonathan gave his weapons to the boy and said, "Go, carry them back to town."

[41]After the boy had gone, David got up from the south side of the stone and bowed down before Jonathan three times, with his face to the ground. Then they kissed each other and wept together—but David wept the most.

⁴²Jonathan said to David, "Go in peace, for we have sworn friendship with each other in the name of the LORD, saying, 'The LORD is witness between you and me, and between your descendants and my descendants forever.'" Then David left, and Jonathan went back to the town.

---

1. Saul said that David had to be eliminated to insure Jonathan's succession to the throne. How did Saul demonstrate that Jonathan's kingship was not his chief concern (vv. 30-33)?

---

2. What reasons would Jonathan have had to be envious of David?

---

3. Why do you think Jonathan chose to see David as a friend rather than as a rival?

4. Put yourself in the place of David, waiting out there in the field for two days (1 Samuel 20:24-27). How might your thoughts turn to envy of Jonathan?

5. If David had let envious thoughts run away with him, what might he have done when Jonathan came to shoot arrows in the field (v. 35)?

6. How did David and Jonathan demonstrate the depth of their compassion for each other (vv. 34-42)?

7. David and Jonathan both wept, but why do you think David "wept the most" (v. 41)?

8. In order for compassion to overcome envy, what must happen in a person's heart?

9. In your own experience, when has God turned envy of another person into compassion for that person, and how did it happen?

10. Where does the story of David, Jonathan and Saul speak to you most specifically?

COMMIT

■ Consider someone you envy. (If you can honestly say you envy no one, think of someone for whom you have trouble feeling compassion.) Try to see that person through God's eyes. Enumerate all the good and positive qualities of that person.

■ Consider ways that the person you envy (or for whom you feel little compassion) might be suffering from spiritual, emotional or even physical pain. Put yourself in that person's place and notice changes in your attitude.

Pray that you will see yourself and anyone you envy through God's eyes. Pray that compassion will replace envy.

For further reading: *Chapters three and four of* A Heart for God.

From Hatred to Love

Psalm 52

One theme that runs through both the Old and New Testaments is that sin is a serious matter with very serious consequences. It cannot be taken lightly, for its effects are both far-reaching and long-lasting upon our relationship to God, to ourselves and to others. Saul did not begin by hating David; in fact, he loved him. But once Saul became envious of David, his unchecked and unrepentant sin led to murderous hatred.

The worst thing about hatred is that it causes a person to fall away from the love of God and the love of one another. Instead of acting for the ultimate welfare of our neighbor, hate causes us to despise, loathe, be intolerant of and wish malice on others.

What ultimately sets us free to love is when we consider God's extravagant love for us in spite of our shortcomings and moral flaws. What melts our hearts is when we reflect on how time after time God has forgiven us and been tender and patient with us, until we finally learned what he was trying to teach us. How can we harbor malice towards another when the *only* One who is altogether perfect continues to love us despite our sin?

OPEN

■ What are some disguises people use to cover up hatred?

■ Do you feel that love is always stronger than hate? Explain.

 STUDY

Background: Saul relentlessly pursued David with one objective: to destroy him. David sought help from the priest Ahimelech at Nob, northeast of Jerusalem. Unfortunately Doeg the Edomite, a servant of Saul, was there at the same time. Doeg spotted David and informed Saul (1 Samuel 21:1-7, 22:9-10). This psalm expresses David's thoughts and feelings when he realized he had been betrayed.

Read Psalm 52.

¹Why do you boast of evil, you mighty man?
   Why do you boast all day long,
     you who are a disgrace in the eyes of God?

²Your tongue plots destruction;

it is like a sharpened razor,
you who practice deceit.
³You love evil rather than good,
falsehood rather than speaking the truth.

⁴You love every harmful word,
O you deceitful tongue!

⁵Surely God will bring you down to everlasting ruin:
He will snatch you up and tear you from your tent;
he will uproot you from the land of the living.

⁶The righteous will see and fear;
they will laugh at him, saying,
⁷"Here now is the man
who did not make God his stronghold
but trusted in his great wealth
and grew strong by destroying others!"

⁸But I am like an olive tree
flourishing in the house of God;
I trust in God's unfailing love
for ever and ever.
⁹I will praise you forever for what you have done;
in your name I will hope, for your name is good.
I will praise you in the presence of your saints.

---

1. What emotions do you see running through this psalm?

2. Who do you think verses 1-7 are addressing? Why?

3. What are the dominant characteristics of David's enemy (vv. 1-4)?

4. Do you know, or have you known, someone who could be described by verses 1-4? If so, what spiritual struggles has this person caused in your life?

5. How does David see the ultimate fate of his enemy (vv. 5-7)?

6. How does the psalm change between verses 7 and 8?

_____

7. In contrast to the fate of David's enemy, how does David see his own future (vv. 8-9)?

_____

8. How can David be so confident of both the downfall of his enemy and his own bright prospects (vv. 5, 8-9)?

_____

9. Consider this statement: "In Psalm 52, David hates the evil in his enemy but does not hate his enemy." Explain why you agree or disagree.

10. We often hear the advice that we should "hate the sin but love the sinner." What do you think this means in a practical sense?

---

11. Where do you feel you have succeeded in "hating the sin but loving the sinner"?

 COMMIT

- It is difficult for a Christian to admit hatred. We are followers of Christ, who taught us to love others. Bring to the Lord anyone (a person or a group) for whom you have lingering resentment or bitterness. Turn over to the Lord both your enemy and your own attitudes.

- Thank God for his unconditional love for you. Thank him for his unconditional love for your enemies.

Pray for an enemy (Matthew 5:44). If you cannot bring yourself to do that, pray for yourself, that you will better understand and begin to feel empathy for that person. Note that praying for our enemies does not mean we deny any evil they have done.

For further reading: *Chapters five and six of* A Heart for God.

From Rebellion to Submission

1 Samuel 24

Those who take God seriously, who believe God to be who he says he is, are committed to the process of learning to submit and obey. We think to be free means doing it our way. God says true freedom comes from doing it his way. And the fruit that is produced by living in harmony with God is not death but all the things that pertain to life: joy and peace and knowledge and power.

Saul shows us the terrifying results of using our freedom to choose independence from God. By contrast, David shows us that there is a better way to live our lives, and that better way is in obedience and surrender to God. For all of David's passion, giftedness, exuberance and charisma, there was something far deeper still that operated in and through his personality. He truly loved God, and he expressed his love by submitting to God's authority. It is no small thing to consider that a man so compelling, so forceful and so engaging chose to submit to God's rule.

What is the fruit of a life submitted to God? We become like him! One of God's goals is to shape our character so that we will manifest his kindness, mercy, love, purity, wisdom and so on in ways that are reflected through our own distinctive personalities. To put it another way, God is making us holy. But there is a requirement in learning how to submit to God's authority: humility.

 OPEN

- Would you describe yourself as naturally rebellious or naturally submissive? Explain your response.

- In what circumstances do you find it easiest to submit to authority, and why?

 STUDY

Read 1 Samuel 24.

[1]After Saul returned from pursuing the Philistines, he was told, "David is in the Desert of En Gedi." [2]So Saul took three thousand chosen men from all Israel and set out to look for David and his men near the Crags of the Wild Goats.

[3]He came to the sheep pens along the way; a cave was there, and Saul went in to relieve himself. David and his men were far back in the cave. [4]The men said, "This is the day the LORD spoke of when he said to you, 'I will give your enemy into your hands for you to deal

with as you wish.'" Then David crept up unnoticed and cut off a corner of Saul's robe.

⁵Afterward, David was conscience-stricken for having cut off a corner of his robe. ⁶He said to his men, "The LORD forbid that I should do such a thing to my master, the LORD's anointed, or lift my hand against him; for he is the anointed of the LORD." ⁷With these words David rebuked his men and did not allow them to attack Saul. And Saul left the cave and went his way.

⁸Then David went out of the cave and called out to Saul, "My lord the king!" When Saul looked behind him, David bowed down and prostrated himself with his face to the ground. ⁹He said to Saul, "Why do you listen when men say, 'David is bent on harming you'? ¹⁰This day you have seen with your own eyes how the LORD delivered you into my hands in the cave. Some urged me to kill you, but I spared you; I said, 'I will not lift my hand against my master, because he is the LORD's anointed.' ¹¹See, my father, look at this piece of your robe in my hand! I cut off the corner of your robe but did not kill you. Now understand and recognize that I am not guilty of wrongdoing or rebellion. I have not wronged you, but you are hunting me down to take my life. ¹²May the LORD judge between you and me. And may the LORD avenge the wrongs you have done to me, but my hand will not touch you. ¹³As the old saying goes, 'From evildoers come evil deeds,' so my hand will not touch you.

¹⁴"Against whom has the king of Israel come out? Whom are you pursuing? A dead dog? A flea? ¹⁵May the LORD be our judge and decide between us. May he consider my cause and uphold it; may he vindicate me by delivering me from your hand."

¹⁶When David finished saying this, Saul asked, "Is that your voice, David my son?" And he wept aloud. ¹⁷"You are more righteous than I," he said. "You have treated me well, but I have treated you badly.

[18]You have just now told me of the good you did to me; the LORD delivered me into your hands, but you did not kill me. [19]When a man finds his enemy, does he let him get away unharmed? May the LORD reward you well for the way you treated me today. [20]I know that you will surely be king and that the kingdom of Israel will be established in your hands. [21]Now swear to me by the LORD that you will not cut off my descendants or wipe out my name from my father's family."

[22]So David gave his oath to Saul. Then Saul returned home, but David and his men went up to the stronghold.

---

1. David and his men had been running from Saul for some time. What thoughts and feelings would he have struggled with in verses 1-7?

---

2. What justifiable reasons could David have given to kill Saul?

---

3. Why did David refuse to take advantage of the situation and kill his enemy (vv. 6-7)?

4. What qualities must have been in David's heart to allow him to have mercy on Saul?

5. Think of a time when you let an opportunity pass by because you did not feel God leading you to seize it. How did you know, and what have been the long-term results (so far)?

6. Although David chose not to kill Saul, he did give in to the impulse to play a sly trick (v. 4). Why do you think he was "conscience-stricken" afterward (v. 5)?

7. When Saul was safely out of the cave, David did take advantage of his opportunity to do something other than to kill his enemy. How did he make use of the situation (vv. 8-15)?

8. How do David's words to Saul show his submission to God's will?

9. What effect did David's words have on Saul (vv. 16-22)?

10. Since we know that God loves us and has our best interests at heart, why do you think we often find it so difficult to submit to his will?

 COMMIT

■ Where might you be consciously or unconsciously rebelling against God? Think of areas of life where you have not been able to get peace or reassurance. Pray that the Holy Spirit will gently reveal your attitudes and help you submit to God's will.

Thank God for his gracious gift of repentance and for the way he welcomes us back to himself through Christ.

For further reading: Chapters seven and eight of A Heart for God.

From Anger to Meekness
1 Samuel 25:18-35

Of all the emotions, anger is one of the most common and most powerful. It's considered one of the so-called deadly sins, and for a very good reason: anger can be murderous. One of the most dangerous elements of anger is the feeling of being entirely justified in expressing outrageous behavior.

Of course anger can be more of a problem for one person than another. Few of us, however, are completely free of its grip. Yet anger *is* under our power to control. Once having found the reason or motive for our anger, then we must learn to release it in a healthy way.

The remedy for anger is meekness. To be meek in the biblical sense of the term is to be anything but weak. The meaning of meekness is closer to the image of a powerful stallion surging with energy, pulsating with vitality, but *tamed*—a majestic creature that has learned to obey its master's command through a small tug on the reins.

It is when the capacity to use force is the greatest that the choice not to do so can be the most constructive. Meekness does not seek to harm but to work for peace.

When the wealthy sheep farmer Nabal offended David, David was tempted to explode in anger. If David shows us how not to deal with anger, and Nabal shows us how not to treat people, Nabal's wife Abigail is a model of how to do both things right.

 OPEN

■ Identify three or four good reasons to be angry.

■ What are some healthy channels for releasing anger?

 STUDY

Background: After the prophet Samuel died and the last bit of moral restraint in Saul seemed to disappear, David and his men moved out of Judah to the desert. They found themselves near the property of a very wealthy man, Nabal, whose name means "Fool." David decided to provide protection for Nabal's flocks of goats and sheep. At sheep-shearing time, David expected to receive something in return for protecting Nabal's property. Nabal refused—with insults. David's response was immediate and harsh. Fortunately, the foolish Nabal had a wise wife named Abigail who intervened.

Read 1 Samuel 25:18-35.

[18]Abigail lost no time. She took two hundred loaves of bread, two skins of wine, five dressed sheep, five seahs of roasted grain, a hundred cakes of raisins and two hundred cakes of pressed figs, and loaded them on donkeys. [19]Then she told her servants, "Go on ahead; I'll follow you." But she did not tell her husband Nabal.

[20]As she came riding her donkey into a mountain ravine, there were David and his men descending toward her, and she met them. [21]David had just said, "It's been useless—all my watching over this fellow's property in the desert so that nothing of his was missing. He has paid me back evil for good. [22]May God deal with David, be it ever so severely, if by morning I leave alive one male of all who belong to him!"

[23]When Abigail saw David, she quickly got off her donkey and bowed down before David with her face to the ground. [24]She fell at his feet and said: "My lord, let the blame be on me alone. Please let your servant speak to you; hear what your servant has to say. [25]May my lord pay no attention to that wicked man Nabal. He is just like his name—his name is Fool, and folly goes with him. But as for me, your servant, I did not see the men my master sent.

[26]"Now since the LORD has kept you, my master, from bloodshed and from avenging yourself with your own hands, as surely as the LORD lives and as you live, may your enemies and all who intend to harm my master be like Nabal. [27]And let this gift, which your servant has brought to my master, be given to the men who follow you. [28]Please forgive your servant's offense, for the LORD will certainly make a lasting dynasty for my master, because he fights the LORD's battles. Let no wrongdoing be found in you as long as you live. [29]Even though someone is pursuing you to take your life, the life of my master will be bound securely in the bundle of the living by the LORD your God. But the lives of your enemies he will hurl away as

from the pocket of a sling. ³⁰When the LORD has done for my master every good thing he promised concerning him and has appointed him leader over Israel, ³¹my master will not have on his conscience the staggering burden of needless bloodshed or of having avenged himself. And when the LORD has brought my master success, re-member your servant."

³²David said to Abigail, "Praise be to the LORD, the God of Israel, who has sent you today to meet me. ³³May you be blessed for your good judgment and for keeping me from bloodshed this day and from avenging myself with my own hands. ³⁴Otherwise, as surely as the LORD, the God of Israel, lives, who has kept me from harming you, if you had not come quickly to meet me, not one male belonging to Nabal would have been left alive by daybreak."

³⁵Then David accepted from her hand what she had brought him and said, "Go home in peace. I have heard your words and granted your request."

---

1. How would you describe Abigail's strategy for taming David's anger?

---

2. In response to Nabal's refusal, what did David plan to do (vv. 21-22)?

3. Do you think David's anger was reasonable or excessive? Why?
   (For further background, scan vv. 4-17.)

4. What would make Abigail's words in verse 26 especially powerful
   to restrain David's rage?

5. How would Abigail's gift of food help to defuse the situation (vv.
   18, 27)?

6. As Abigail continued her appeal (vv. 28-31), what wise advice did
   she offer, and in what spirit?

7. Contrast David's mood in verses 32-35 with his mood only minutes before in verses 21-22. How has his outlook on the situation changed?

8. When you have been angry, has anyone ever intervened with you as Abigail did with David? If so, what was the outcome?

9. What does it take to set anger aside as David did here?

10. How does the story of David and Abigail give you a different perspective on your own times of anger?

COMMIT

- In what areas of life are you most prone to lash out in anger? If an "Abigail" came to reason with you, how would she make her appeal?

  What does that tell you about how you could more effectively manage your own anger?

- Where can you serve as an "Abigail" for someone else?

Thank God for times he has sent someone to intervene and has prevented anger from leading you into foolishness.

For further reading: *Chapters nine and ten of* A Heart for God.

From Despair to Hope

Psalm 18:1-6, 16-19, 46-50

All noble things are difficult. God is doing the same work in our lives that he was doing in David's life—bringing us into glory and making us suitable for heaven. He did not shield David from the requirements of becoming spiritually mature, and neither will he shield us.

Christians are people of hope and not despair. We know that God had the first word and will also have the last. David is a wonderful example of the fact that hope is inseparable from faith in the true God. David knew that God was trustworthy, loving, holy and just. He knew that God's goodness could never be exhausted. And the fruit of David's hope in God was that it gave him patience to wait and a steadfastness that probably wasn't natural to his temperament.

David's hope also enabled him to suffer honestly but well. He did not expect life always to be easy or even fair. But these difficulties were seen as occasions for God's grace and help. If we likewise accept the fact that life is not always fair and that it can be difficult, we will be able to live from faithful strength instead of from frightened anxiety.

OPEN

- What would you say to a person who tells you he or she has no hope?

What would you *not* say?

STUDY

Read Psalm 18:1-6, 16-19, 46-50.

For the director of music. Of David the servant of the LORD. He sang to the LORD the words of this song when the LORD delivered him from the hand of all his enemies and from the hand of Saul. He said:

^{1}I love you, O LORD, my strength.

^{2}The LORD is my rock, my fortress and my deliverer;
    my God is my rock, in whom I take refuge.
    He is my shield and the horn of my salvation, my stronghold.
^{3}I call to the LORD, who is worthy of praise,
    and I am saved from my enemies.

⁴The cords of death entangled me;
    the torrents of destruction overwhelmed me.
⁵The cords of the grave coiled around me;
    the snares of death confronted me.
⁶In my distress I called to the LORD;
    I cried to my God for help.
From his temple he heard my voice;
    my cry came before him, into his ears.

¹⁶He reached down from on high and took hold of me;
    he drew me out of deep waters.
¹⁷He rescued me from my powerful enemy,
    from my foes, who were too strong for me.
¹⁸They confronted me in the day of my disaster,
    but the LORD was my support.
¹⁹He brought me out into a spacious place;
    he rescued me because he delighted in me.

⁴⁶The LORD lives! Praise be to my Rock!
    Exalted be God my Savior!
⁴⁷He is the God who avenges me,
    who subdues nations under me,
      ⁴⁸who saves me from my enemies.
You exalted me above my foes;
    from violent men you rescued me.
⁴⁹Therefore I will praise you among the nations, O LORD;
    I will sing praises to your name.
⁵⁰He gives his king great victories;
    he shows unfailing kindness to his anointed,
    to David and his descendants forever.

1. In what terms does David describe the Lord in verses 1-3?

2. Why would David have had reason to despair (vv. 4-5)?

3. *Entangled, overwhelmed, coiled around, confronted* . . . these are powerful words (vv. 4- 5) to describe threats to one's very life and soul. In what circumstances have you felt as David did? (A person does not have to be threatened with physical death to feel set upon in these ways.)

4. David writes, "In my distress I called to the LORD; I cried to my God for help" (v. 6). Why do you think we so often neglect to cry out to God, or at least postpone doing so, when we are in trouble?

5. How had the Lord proved himself faithful to David (vv. 6, 16-19)?

6. David was a skillful warrior and a master strategist both politically and militarily. In light of his talents, why are verses 16-19 remarkable?

7. As David brings his victory song to a conclusion, how does he see his future (vv. 46-50)?

8. What brought David from the point of despair to the point of hope?

9. Which of your past experiences with God gives you the most hope for the future?

COMMIT

- Consider all the reasons you need hope right now. What do you hope for, and why?

- David's situation often looked hopeless, yet he found reason to hope in God, and God answered him. Cry out to God for help as David did. Watch for ways in which God is reaching down to draw you out of "deep waters" (v. 16).

Thank God for our hope of eternal life in Christ. Pray that you will be able to let God lift your spirits when you doubt and that he will fill you with godly hope.

For further reading: *Chapters eleven and twelve of* A Heart for God.

GUIDELINES FOR LEADERS

Leading a Bible discussion can be an enjoyable and rewarding experience. But it can also be intimidating—especially if you've never done it before. If this is how you feel, you're in good company.

Remember when God asked Moses to lead the Israelites out of Egypt? Moses replied, "O Lord, please send someone else to do it" (Ex 4:13). But God gave Moses the help (human and divine) he needed to be a strong leader.

Leading a Bible discussion is not difficult if you follow certain guidelines. You don't need to be an expert on the Bible or a trained teacher. The suggestions listed below can help you to effectively fulfill your role as leader—and enjoy doing it.

PREPARING FOR THE STUDY

1. As you study the passage ahead of time, ask God to help you understand it and apply it in your own life. Unless this happens, you will not be prepared to lead others. Pray too for the various members of the group. Ask God to open your hearts to the message of his Word and motivate you to action.

2. Read the introduction to the entire guide to get an overview of the subject at hand and the issues that will be explored.

3. Be ready for the "Open" questions with a personal story or example. The group will be only as vulnerable and open as its leader.

4. Read the chapter of the companion book that is suggested under "Further Reading" at the end of each study.

5. As you begin preparing for each study, read and reread the assigned Bible passage to familiarize yourself with it. You may want to look up the passage in a Bible so that you can see its context.

6. This study guide is based on the New International Version of the Bible. That is what is reproduced in your guide. It will help you and the group if you use this translation as the basis for your study and discussion.

7. Carefully work through each question in the study. Spend time in meditation and reflection as you consider how to respond.

8. Write your thoughts and responses in the space provided in the study guide. This will help you to express your understanding of the passage clearly.

9. It might help you to have a Bible dictionary handy. Use it to look up any unfamiliar words, names or places.

10. Take the final (application) questions and the "Commit" portion of each study seriously. Consider what this means for your life, what changes you may need to make in your lifestyle and/or what actions you can take in your church or with people you know. Remember that the group will follow your lead in responding to the studies.

LEADING THE STUDY

1. Be sure everyone in your group has a study guide and Bible. Encourage the group to prepare beforehand for each discussion by

reading the introduction to the guide and by working through the questions in the study.

2. At the beginning of your first time together, explain that these studies are meant to be discussions, not lectures. Encourage the members of the group to participate. However, do not put pressure on those who may be hesitant to speak during the first few sessions.

3. Begin the study on time. Open with prayer, asking God to help the group understand and apply the passage.

4. Have a group member read the introductory paragraph at the beginning of the discussion. This will remind the group of the topic of the study.

5. Every study begins with a section called "Open." These "approach" questions are meant to be asked before the passage is read. They are important for several reasons.

First, there is always a stiffness that needs to be overcome before people will begin to talk openly. A good question will break the ice.

Second, most people will have lots of different things going on in their minds (dinner, an exam, an important meeting coming up, how to get the car fixed) that have nothing to do with the study. A creative question will get their attention and draw them into the discussion.

Third, approach questions can reveal where our thoughts or feelings need to be transformed by Scripture. That is why it is especially important not to read the passage before the approach question is asked. The passage will tend to color the honest reactions people would otherwise give, because they feel they are supposed to think the way the Bible does.

6. Have a group member read aloud the passage to be studied.

7. As you ask the questions, keep in mind that they are designed to be used just as they are written. You may simply read them aloud. Or you may prefer to express them in your own words.

   There may be times when it is appropriate to deviate from the study guide. For example, a question may already have been answered. If so, move on to the next question. Or someone may raise an important question not covered in the guide. Take time to discuss it, but try to keep the group from going off on tangents.

8. Avoid answering your own questions. Repeat or rephrase them if necessary until they are clearly understood. An eager group quickly becomes passive and silent if members think the leader will give all the *right* answers.

9. Don't be afraid of silence. People may need time to think about the question before formulating their answers.

10. Don't be content with just one answer. Ask, "What do the rest of you think?" or, "Anything else?" until several people have given answers to a question.

11. Acknowledge all contributions. Be affirming whenever possible. Never reject an answer. If it is clearly off-base, ask, "Which verse led you to that conclusion?" or, "What do the rest of you think?"

12. Don't expect every answer to be addressed to you, even though this will probably happen at first. As group members become more at ease, they will begin to truly interact with each other. This is one sign of healthy discussion.

13. Don't be afraid of controversy. It can be stimulating! If you don't resolve an issue completely, don't be frustrated. Move on and keep it in mind for later. A subsequent study may solve the problem.

14. Periodically summarize what the group has said about the passage. This helps to draw together the various ideas mentioned and gives continuity to the study. But don't preach.

15. Don't skip over the application questions at the end of each study. It's important that we each apply the message of the passage to ourselves in a specific way. Be willing to get things started by describing how you have been affected by the study.

   Depending on the makeup of your group and the length of time you've been together, you may or may not want to discuss the "Commit" section. If not, allow the group to read it and reflect on it silently. Encourage members to make specific commitments and to write them in their study guide. Ask them the following week how they did with their commitments.

16. Conclude your time together with conversational prayer. Ask for God's help in following through on the commitments you've made.

17. End on time.

Many more suggestions and helps are found in The Big Book on Small Groups *by Jeffrey Arnold.*

S T U D Y   N O T E S

Study One. FROM FEAR TO FAITH. 1 Samuel 17:1-50.

Purpose: To rely on the Lord's strength to conquer fear.

Question 1. "The text undoubtedly wants to display Saul's incompetence. The people had sought a king to lead their armies into battle. It was not odd, however, for a king to send out a champion rather than going himself. Even in the event that the king was a great warrior, others would be given the opportunity to prove their skills first. In some senses it would resemble all of the preliminary bouts that precede the 'main event' in boxing" (John H. Walton, ed., *The IVP Bible Background Commentary: Old Testament* [Downers Grove, Ill.: InterVarsity Press, 2000], p. 307).

Question 2. The "bronze greaves" which Goliath wore on his legs (v. 6) were "a protective covering about the shank of the leg. The only occurrence of the word is at I Sam. 17:6, where the armor of Goliath is described" (J. W. Wevers, "Greaves," in *Interpreter's Dictionary of the Bible* [Nashville: Abingdon, 1962], 2:473).

Question 4. David was already in the service of King Saul. Saul was subject to oppression by an evil spirit, and at those times David would play his harp and soothe Saul (1 Sam 16:14-23). David did not live in Saul's palace full-time, but "went back and forth from Saul to tend his father's sheep in Bethlehem" (1 Sam 17:15). Unknown to Saul, the prophet Samuel had anointed David as the next king of Israel, Saul's replacement (1 Sam 16:1-13).

Question 6. Concerning Saul's armor (vv. 38-39): "The king's tunic and armor would have been very distinctive. If David went out dressed in them, many would have thought that the king himself was going out. Perhaps such a misidentification would have seemed attractive to Saul, who had been sought out by the Israelites to lead them forth into battle. . . . David's refusal would have reflected his recognition that without being trained on how to use the armor and weapons to his advantage, they would become a detriment" (*IVP Bible Background Commentary: Old Testament*, p. 308).

Study Two.   FROM ENVY TO COMPASSION.
1 Samuel 20:30-42.

Purpose: To reject envy and to choose compassion.

Open. Don't give the details about the situation where someone envied you. Just talk about your thoughts and feelings in that situation.

Question 1. Saul tried to kill Jonathan—which would have put an end to Jonathan's place in the succession! Saul did have two other sons (1 Sam 14:49) but it is doubtful that he had them in mind when he threw the spear. (All three sons would later die with their father in battle with the Philistines.)

Question 2. Saul was correct that if David lived, Jonathan would never rule Israel. David, not Jonathan, was God's choice as the next king. Even if Jonathan did not know that the prophet Samuel had anointed David, he could tell that his father saw David as a contender for the throne.

Question 3. Jonathan saw himself accurately before God. God is the Creator and Lord; Jonathan was the creature. God was in control of his destiny. Therefore, being a king wasn't a possession he could control, but a gift that only God could give. What a contrast to his father! If God was indeed in charge, Jonathan could celebrate David's victory without looking over his shoulder. Why should he worry about David's success, knowing that the Lord God was looking out for both of them?

Question 4. Jonathan could come and go freely to the royal palace and his father's presence, while David had to hide to save his own life. Though David was God's choice as king, and though he had done nothing against Saul, Saul naturally favored Jonathan.

Question 5. David might have decided that Jonathan would turn traitor to save his own kingdom. David could have distrusted the signal, run away without meeting Jonathan, or even tried to kill Jonathan in supposed self-defense!

Study Three.   FROM HATRED TO LOVE. Psalm 52.

Purpose: To let love overcome hatred in our hearts and actions.

Question 2. David may have meant Doeg, since his betrayal was the impetus for this psalm. However, Doeg's position as Saul's head shepherd (1 Sam 21:7) hardly qualifies him as a "mighty man" (v. 1) unless David meant the term sarcastically. Saul is a more likely candidate; verses 1-3 portray someone consumed with plotting harm, as Saul was toward David. Or perhaps this evil man symbolized all David's enemies, who were ultimately the enemies of God.